Everyone Eats

All Children Reading Cambodia
Illustrated by Chhuon Sambte

Library For All Ltd.

Library For All is an Australian not for profit organisation with a mission to make knowledge accessible to all via an innovative digital library solution. Visit us at libraryforall.org

Everyone Eats

This edition published 2022

Published by Library For All Ltd
Email: info@libraryforall.org
URL: libraryforall.org

Library For All gratefully acknowledges the contributions of all who made previous editions of this book possible.

The Asia Foundation

This work is a modified version of the original story, ©The Asia Foundation.
Released under CC BY 4.0.

Original illustrations by Chhuon Sambte

Everyone Eats
All Children Reading Cambodia
ISBN: 978-1-922918-97-0
SKU03045

Everyone Eats

This is a cow.

The cow eats grass.

3

This is a chicken.

The chicken eats corn.

This is a horse.

The horse eats a banana tree.

7

This is an elephant.

The elephant eats
sugarcane.

This is a lion.

The lion eats raw meat.

They all live by eating food.

But the lion's food is different. The lion eats meat while the other animals eat plants.

You can use these questions to talk about this book with your family, friends and teachers.

What did you learn from this book?

Describe this book in one word. Funny? Scary? Colourful? Interesting?

How did this book make you feel when you finished reading it?

What was your favourite part of this book?

download our reader app
getlibraryforall.org

About the contributors

Library For All works with authors and illustrators from around the world to develop diverse, relevant, high quality stories for young readers. Visit libraryforall.org for the latest news on writers' workshop events, submission guidelines and other creative opportunities.

Did you enjoy this book?

We have hundreds more expertly curated original stories to choose from.

We work in partnership with authors, educators, cultural advisors, governments and NGOs to bring the joy of reading to children everywhere.

Did you know?

We create global impact in these fields by embracing the United Nations Sustainable Development Goals.